Letts
KS1
Success
Workbook

Paul Broadbent

Maths
SATs

Contents

Numbers

Calculations

Shapes and measures

Graphs and charts

National Test practice and glossary

Answers

See answer booklet

Counting patterns

Counting objects

Draw circles round these bugs to group them into 2s. Write down how many groups there are, and how many bugs altogether.

_____ groups of 2 = _____ bugs

Counting to 100

This number square has some numbers missing.

Write in all the missing numbers.

0	1	2	3	4			7		9
10	11				15	16		18	19
	21		23		25		27	28	
30		32	33	34		36		38	
		42			45		47	48	49
50	51			54	55	56			
	61		63					68	69
	71		73	74	75		77		79
		82		84		86		88	
90		92		94	95				99

Sequences

Write down the missing numbers in these sequences.

1 17   18   ☐   ☐   21   22   23   ☐

2 46   ☐   48   49   ☐   ☐   52   ☐

3 32   31   ☐   29   ☐   ☐   26   ☐

4 ☐   ☐   84   83   ☐   81   ☐   ☐

Top Tip Look carefully at the numbers you are given. Start by working out the numbers next to these and then find out the others.

Number patterns

1 Counting in 2s, show the jumps and circle the numbers.

⓪ 1 ② 3 ④ 5 6 7 8 9 10 11 12 13 14 15 16 17 18 19 20

2 Counting in 5s, write the next four numbers.

(15)——(20)——(25)——( )——( )——( )——( )

3 Counting in 3s, write the next four numbers.

(3)——(6)——(9)——( )——( )——( )——( )

I might make some of these bugs go missing – into Mel's bed!

Oh no, I hate bugs!

5

Reading and writing numbers

Teen numbers

Write these numbers as words to find a hidden number.

16

12

14

17

13

19

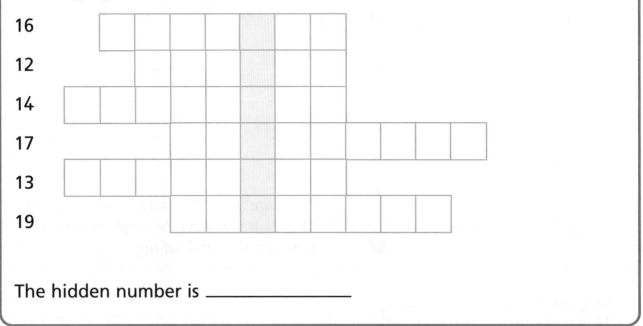

The hidden number is _____

2-digit numbers

Write down the numbers shown by each abacus.

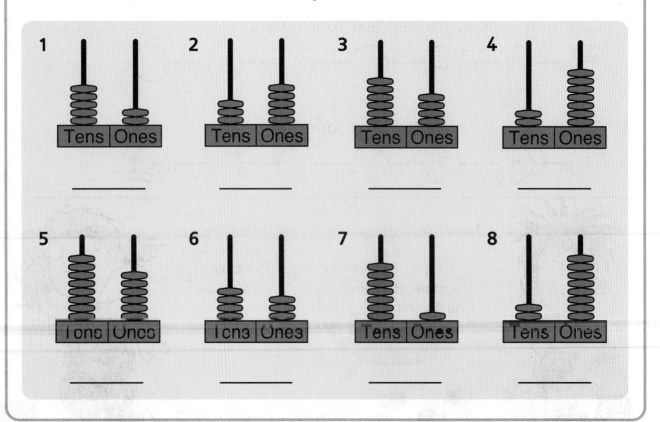

1 Tens | Ones

_____

2 Tens | Ones

_____

3 Tens | Ones

_____

4 Tens | Ones

_____

5 Tens | Ones

_____

6 Tens | Ones

_____

7 Tens | Ones

_____

8 Tens | Ones

_____

3-digit numbers

Fill in the missing numbers.

1 487 = 400 + 80 + ☐

2 394 = 300 + ☐ + 4

3 269 = ☐ + 60 + ☐

4 735 = ☐ + ☐ + 5

5 918 = ☐ + ☐ + ☐

6 842 = ☐ + ☐ + ☐

Odd and even numbers

Circle all the even numbers.

54   18   32

31   47

50

26   25

Top Tip *Remember that even numbers are all multiples of 2. The last digit of an even number is always 0, 2, 4, 6 or 8.*

Multiples

Write the numbers from 1 to 40 in the correct place on this Carroll diagram. The first few numbers have been written in for you.

What do you notice about the numbers here?

If you have not got enough room here, copy the table onto a spare piece of paper.

	multiple of 2	not a multiple of 2
multiple of 5		5
not a multiple of 5	2 4	1 3

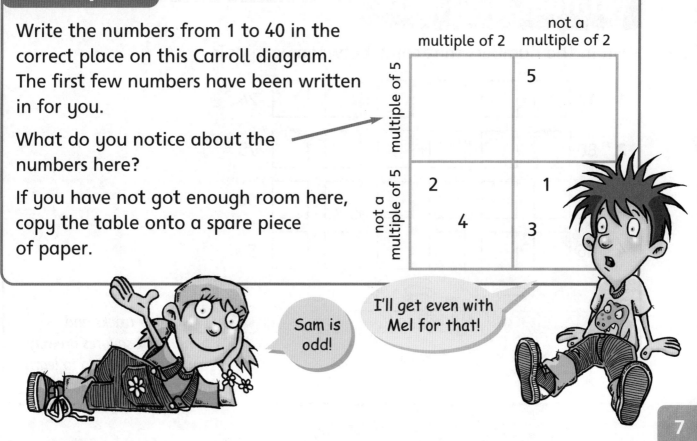

Sam is odd!

I'll get even with Mel for that!

Comparing and ordering

Positions

Draw a line to join each position to the correct car.

Number sequences

Fill in the numbers that come between each pair.

1 17 ☐ ☐ ☐ ☐ ☐ ☐ 24

2 80 ☐ ☐ ☐ ☐ ☐ ☐ 73

3 43 ☐ ☐ ☐ ☐ ☐ ☐ 50

4 66 ☐ ☐ ☐ ☐ ☐ ☐ 59

Top Tip

Number tracks and hundred squares are very useful for helping to learn the order of numbers.

Ordering numbers

Write these sets of numbers in order, starting with the smallest.

1
| 27 | 24 | 30 | 31 | 25 | 19 |

____ ____ ____ ____ ____ ____

2
| 58 | 85 | 47 | 52 | 83 | 60 |

____ ____ ____ ____ ____ ____

Comparing numbers

Circle the bigger number in each pair.

1 34 43   **2** 81 79   **3** 92 95   **4** 68 86

5 57 64   **6** 19 91   **7** 72 69   **8** 87 84

Halfway numbers

Fill in the number in the middle of each pair.

1 17 ☐ 25   **3** 32 ☐ 38

2 51 ☐ 57   **4** 14 ☐ 26

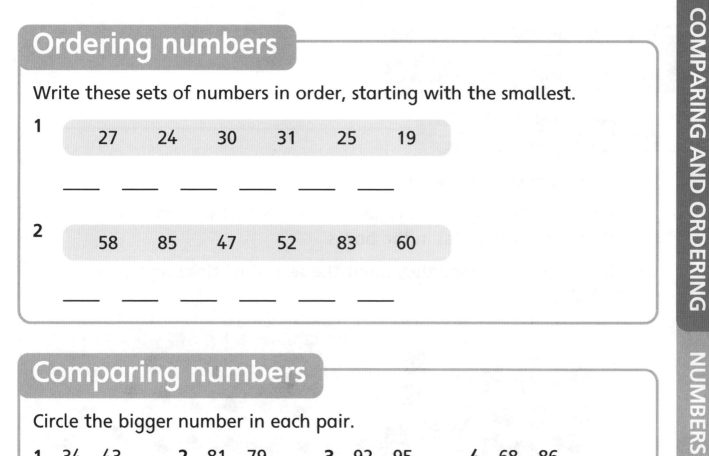

We've been playing golf and I had more shots than Mel.

That means I came first with the lowest score!

Estimating

Good estimates

- Look at each of these sets.

- Without counting them, estimate how many there are in each set. Write your estimates in the boxes.

- Once you have done this, count the sets. How close was your estimate?

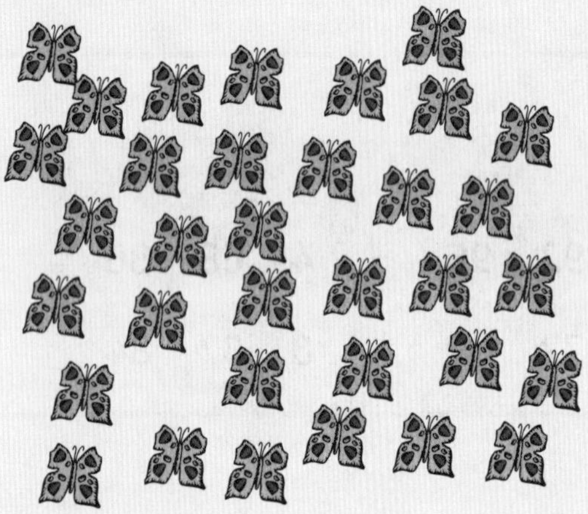

Estimate _____
Count _____

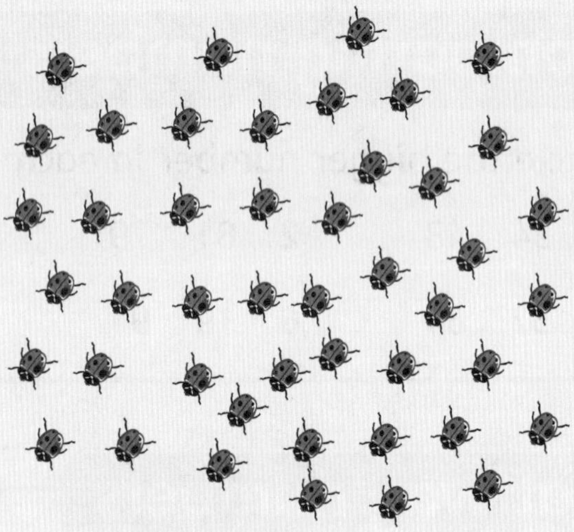

Estimate _____
Count _____

Estimate _____
Count _____

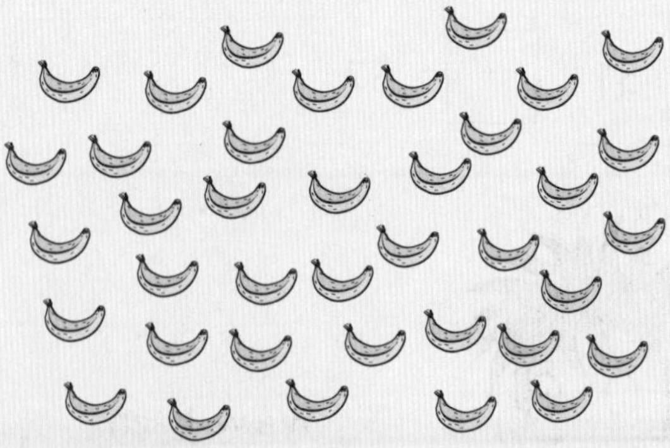

Estimate _____
Count _____

Number lines

Estimate the number shown by each arrow. Write your estimates in the boxes.

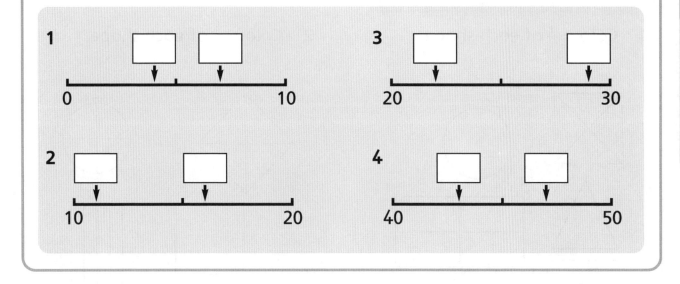

1
0 [ ]↓ [ ]↓ 10

3
20 [ ]↓ [ ]↓ 30

2
[ ]↓ 10 [ ]↓ 20

4
40 [ ]↓ [ ]↓ 50

Rounding

Round these amounts to the nearest 10p. Write the amounts in the correct bags.

63p   57p   71p   81p   66p   84p   65p   76p   55p

Round to 60   Round to 70   Round to 80

Top Tip — *If a number ends in 5 or more, it rounds up to the next 10. If it is less than 5, it rounds down and the 10 stays the same.*

Sam owes me 22p.

I think I'll round that down to 20p!

Fractions

Fractions of shapes

1   Colour $\frac{1}{2}$ of each shape.

2   Colour $\frac{1}{4}$ of each shape.

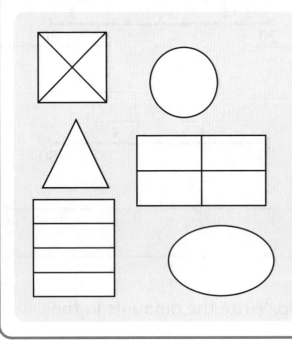

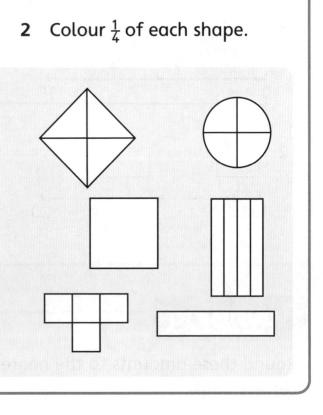

Equal parts

Tick the shapes that show quarters.

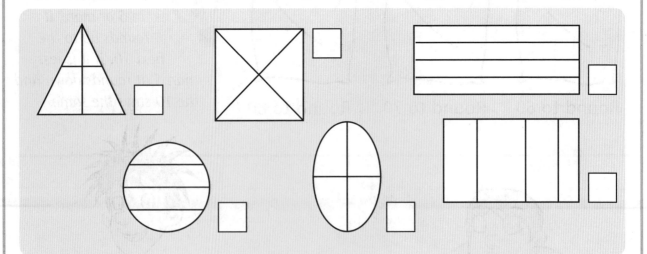

Remember, if a shape is cut into quarters, it is cut into 4 equal parts.

Fractions of amounts

Write down $\frac{1}{2}$ of each of these numbers.
Colour the sweets to help you.

1 $\frac{1}{2}$ of 6 = ☐

2 $\frac{1}{2}$ of 10 = ☐

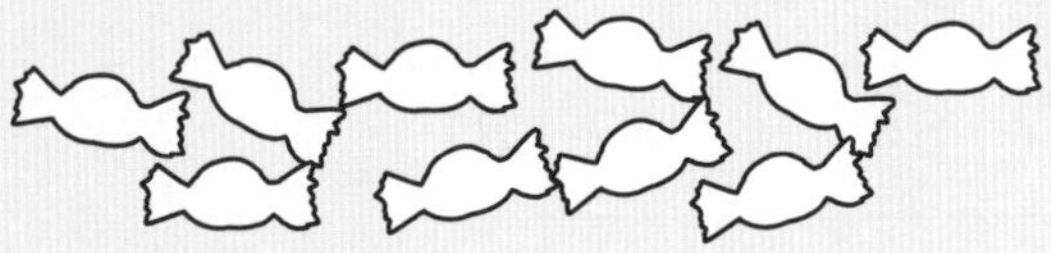

3 $\frac{1}{2}$ of 8 = ☐

4 $\frac{1}{2}$ of 12 = ☐

Write down $\frac{1}{4}$ of each of these numbers.
Colour the sweets to help you.

5 $\frac{1}{4}$ of 8 = ☐

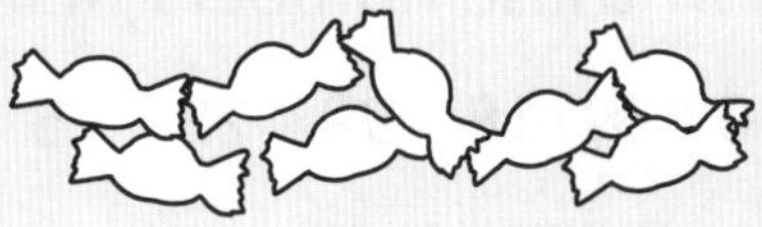

6 $\frac{1}{4}$ of 12 = ☐

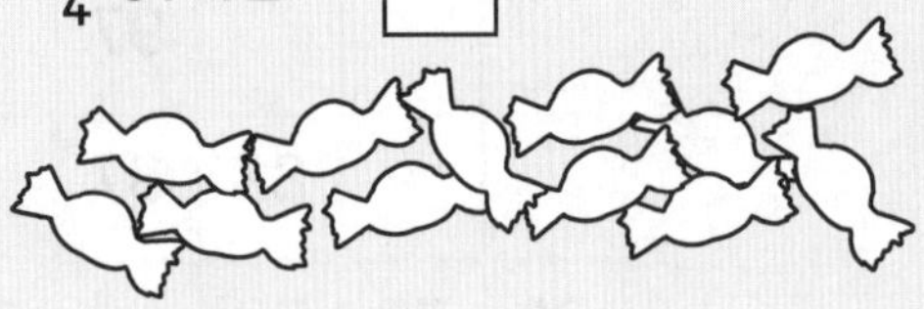

7 $\frac{1}{4}$ of 20 = ☐

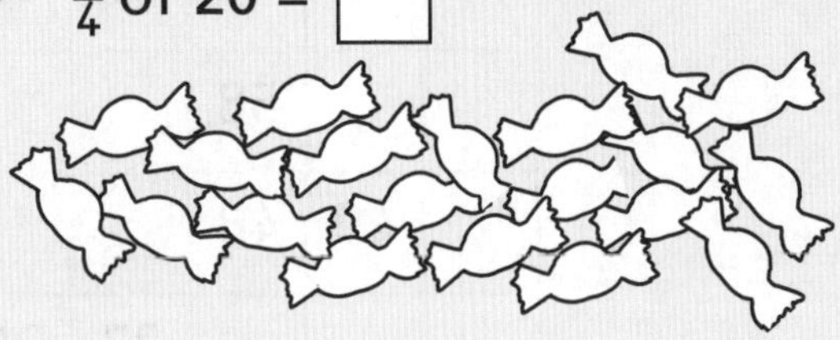

8 $\frac{1}{4}$ of 16 = ☐

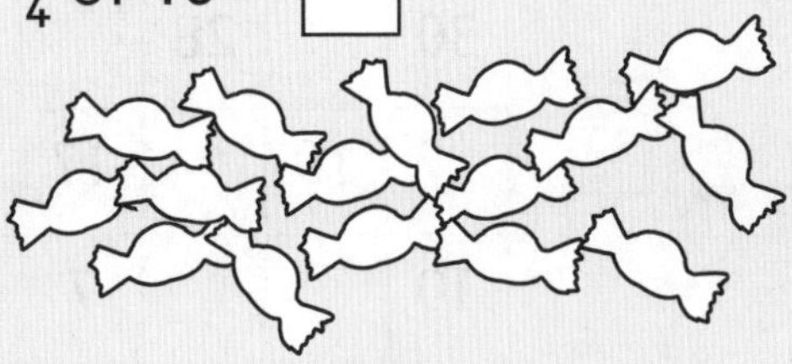

Mel, I have 12 sweets. Would you like a $\frac{1}{4}$ of them?

Give me $\frac{1}{2}$ a minute to work this out...

Numbers investigation

Complete the square

This 100-square is a little different to normal.

- Write in these numbers first:

  39 60 9 18 99 25 75 56

- Now write in all the other numbers to complete the square.

			97		95	94	93		
		88	87			84		82	81
80	79	78		76					
70			67	66			63		61
		58				54	53		51
	49	48			45			42	41
			37	36	35				
30		28				24		22	
	19		17				13		11
10			7	6		4	3	2	1

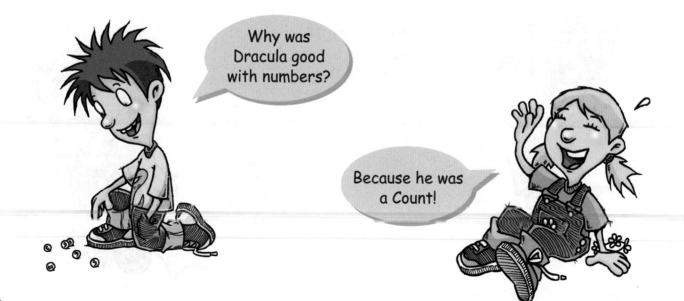

Why was Dracula good with numbers?

Because he was a Count!

And this one!

Here is another 100-square that is a bit different.

- Write in these numbers first:

  73 37 98 23 8 52 14 65

- Now complete the square by writing in all the other numbers.

1	20		40			61			100
2	19	22		42		62	79	82	
3			38		58	63		83	
		24		44			77	84	
	16		36					85	
6	15	26					75		95
7		27		47	54				
			33					88	93
	12		32			69			
10	11	30		50	51	70	71		91

Studying the squares

For both 100-squares:

- Colour in the even numbers.
- Look at the patterns on each of them.

Top Tip

Remember, even numbers always end in the digits 0, 2, 4, 6 or 8.

15

Number facts

Totals to 10

Look at the number in the centre of each circle. Now fill in the boxes to make this number in different ways.

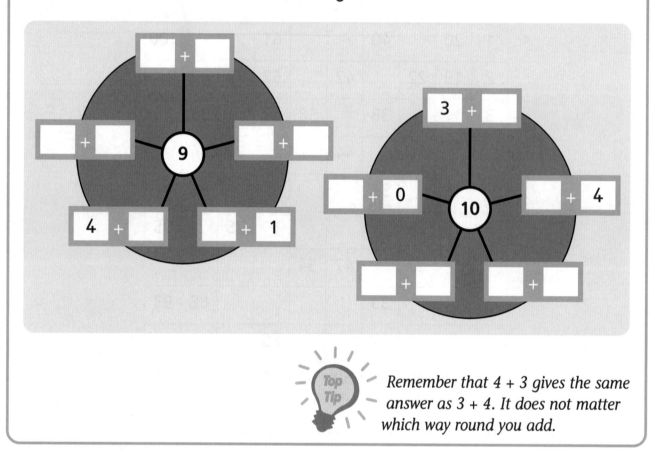

Top Tip — *Remember that 4 + 3 gives the same answer as 3 + 4. It does not matter which way round you add.*

Trios

These trios make different number facts. Fill in each of the facts with the numbers given.

1 4 11 7   4 + ____ = 11   11 − ____ = 4

  7 + ____ = ____   ____ − 4 = ____

2 8 14 6   ____ + ____ = ____   ____ − ____ = ____

  ____ + ____ = ____   ____ − ____ = ____

3 9 16 7   ____ + ____ = ____   ____ − ____ = ____

  ____ + ____ = ____   ____ − ____ = ____

Number bonds

Write down the answers to each of these questions. Then use the code to find five vegetables.

CODE	N	P	O	A	S	I	C	U	R	T
	8	9	10	11	12	13	14	15	16	17

1 $9 + 5 =$ ___   ___

$18 - 7 =$ ___   ___

$8 + 8 =$ ___   ___

$11 + 5 =$ ___   ___

$19 - 9 =$ ___   ___

$8 + 9 =$ ___   ___

2 $11 + 6 =$ ___   ___

$7 + 8 =$ ___   ___

$9 + 7 =$ ___   ___

$14 - 6 =$ ___   ___

$18 - 5 =$ ___   ___

$17 - 8 =$ ___   ___

3 $14 - 5 =$ ___   ___

$6 + 4 =$ ___   ___

$12 + 5 =$ ___   ___

$17 - 6 =$ ___   ___

$13 + 4 =$ ___   ___

$18 - 8 =$ ___   ___

4 $18 - 6 =$ ___   ___

$20 - 11 =$ ___   ___

$7 + 9 =$ ___   ___

$3 + 7 =$ ___   ___

$9 + 6 =$ ___   ___

$6 + 11 =$ ___   ___

$17 - 5 =$ ___   ___

5 $13 - 4 =$ ___   ___

$20 - 9 =$ ___   ___

$9 + 7 =$ ___   ___

$4 + 8 =$ ___   ___

$17 - 9 =$ ___   ___

$6 + 7 =$ ___   ___

$16 - 7 =$ ___   ___

Addition and subtraction

Big numbers

Complete these number trails by writing in the answer to each sum.

1 10 +40 [ ] → +80 [ ] → −20 [ ] → +50 [ ] → −60 100

2 10 +70 [ ] → −50 [ ] → +90 [ ] → −80 [ ] → +60 100

3 100 +400 [ ] → −200 [ ] → +900 [ ] → +700 [ ] → −900 1000

4 100 +600 [ ] → +100 [ ] → −500 [ ] → −100 [ ] → +800 1000

Using doubles

Write the numbers coming out of the doubling machine. Use these to help answer the questions. Each question has 2 answers.

1 14 doubled = _____   14 + 15 = _____

2 21 doubled = _____   21 + 22 = _____

3 60 doubled = _____   60 + 59 = _____

4 35 doubled = _____   35 + 36 = _____

5 25 doubled = _____   25 + 24 = _____

6 40 doubled = _____   40 + 41 = _____

What would happen if I went into the doubling machine?

Double trouble!

Rounding

Draw a line to join each calculation to the correct answer.

| 14 + 19 | 17 – 9 | 46 – 19 | 23 + 9 | 15 + 9 | 26 – 9 |

| 24 | 27 | 8 | 17 | 32 | 33 |

| 27 – 19 | 42 – 9 | 33 – 9 | 36 – 19 | 13 + 19 | 18 + 9 |

Top Tip *If you need to add or take away 9, round it to 10 to make it easier, e.g. 14–9 is 14–10 and then add 1, which is 5. You can do this to add or take away 19, 29, 39...*

Adding 2-digit numbers

Fill in the answer to each question. Colour the star for any you found easy.

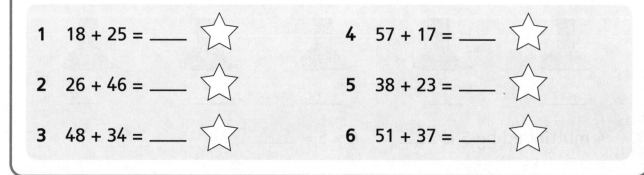

1   18 + 25 = ____   ☆

2   26 + 46 = ____   ☆

3   48 + 34 = ____   ☆

4   57 + 17 = ____   ☆

5   38 + 23 = ____   ☆

6   51 + 37 = ____   ☆

Counting on

Use the number line to help you find the difference between these pairs of numbers. Then write the answers in the boxes.

```
 |................|................|................|
20              30              40              50
```

1   27 to 36 ➔ ____

2   42 to 28 ➔ ____

3   32 to 49 ➔ ____

4   21 to 35 ➔ ____

5   29 to 48 ➔ ____

6   24 to 43 ➔ ____

Multiplication and division

Counting groups

1 Draw 3 fish in each pool. Write the number of fish in each pool beneath it, then fill in the blanks to work out the total number of fish.

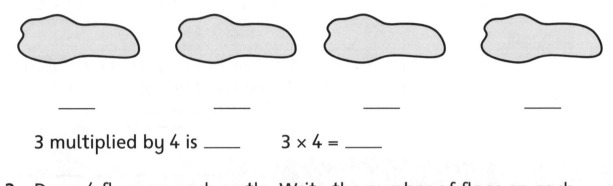

_____   _____   _____   _____

3 multiplied by 4 is ____   3 × 4 = ____

2 Draw 4 flags on each castle. Write the number of flags on each castle beneath it, then fill in the blanks to work out the total number of flags.

_____   _____   _____   _____   _____

4 multiplied by 5 is ____   4 × 5 = ____

Top Tip
The division sign is ÷
Dividing is the opposite to multiplying,
so check your answer with multiplication.
For example: 14 ÷ 2 = 7   2 × 7 = 14

I'm the king of the castle!

I think you're the little rascal!

Dividing

Group these things by circling them, then fill in the missing numbers.

1 Group in 2s

____ groups of 2

12 ÷ 2 = ____

2 Group in 3s

____ groups of 3

15 ÷ 3 = ____

3 Group in 4s

____ groups of 4

16 ÷ 4 = ____

4 Group in 3s

____ groups of 3

12 ÷ 3 = ____

5 Group in 5s

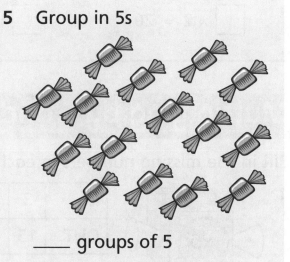

____ groups of 5

15 ÷ 5 = ____

6 Group in 4s

____ groups of 4

12 ÷ 4 = ____

Times tables

2 times table

1   Draw jumps of 2 on this number line. Colour the numbers that you land on.

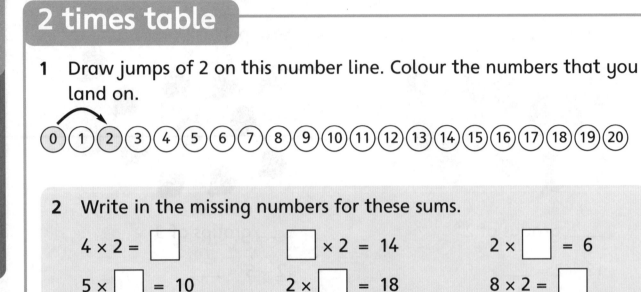

0 1 2 3 4 5 6 7 8 9 10 11 12 13 14 15 16 17 18 19 20

2   Write in the missing numbers for these sums.

4 × 2 = ☐   ☐ × 2 = 14   2 × ☐ = 6

5 × ☐ = 10   2 × ☐ = 18   8 × 2 = ☐

☐ × 2 = 20   ☐ × 2 = 4   2 × ☐ = 12

Multiplying by 5 and 10

Fill in the missing numbers in each table.

1

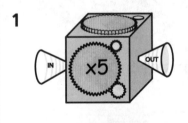

IN	3		8		7		2	
OUT	15	45		25		30		20

2

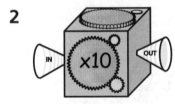

IN	6		4		9		8	
OUT	60	70		50		20		30

Multiplying by 3 and 4

1 Continue to fill in these sequences.

3 6 9 12 □ □ □ □ □ □

4 8 12 16 □ □ □ □ □ □

2 Fill in the missing numbers.

$3 \times \underline{\quad} = 12$ $4 \times \underline{\quad} = 32$ $\underline{\quad} \times 3 = 6$

$5 \times 4 = \underline{\quad}$ $\underline{\quad} \times 7 = 21$ $4 \times \underline{\quad} = 36$

$9 \times \underline{\quad} = 27$ $6 \times \underline{\quad} = 24$ $8 \times 3 = \underline{\quad}$

Tricky tables

Complete these grids by filling in the missing numbers.

1

×	3	2	5
7			
4		8	
9			

2

×	4	10	3
6			
8			
5			

3

×	8	9	7
5			
3			
4			

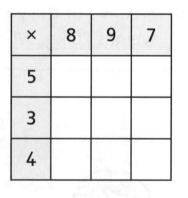

Top Tip

Remember that 2 × 6 gives the same answer as 6 × 2. It does not matter which way round it is written.

Yes – 10 times as messy, 10 times as noisy!

I'm 10 times better at everything than you, Sam!

Problem-solving

Word problems

1 9 bricks, each 10 cm in length, are laid end to end in a row. What is the total length of the row? _____ cm

2 Laura has 28 stickers and Sam has 19 stickers. How many more stickers has Laura than Sam? _____ stickers

3 A football team has 14 players. If 4 players can travel in one car, how many cars are needed to take them to their matches? _____ cars

4 4 egg boxes, each with 6 eggs, are dropped. 15 eggs are broken. How many eggs are left? _____ eggs

5 There are 25 sweets in a bag. Josh eats 6 sweets and Ryan eats twice as many as Josh. How many sweets are left? _____ sweets

6 Fred is $\frac{1}{5}$ of the weight of his Dad, who weighs 70 kg. What does Fred weigh? _____ kg

I'm richer than you. I've got 3 coins and you've only got 1!

No, I'm richer because your three 20p coins only add up to 60p. My £1 coin is worth 100p.

Money totals

Total these coins. First write them as pounds, then write them as pence.

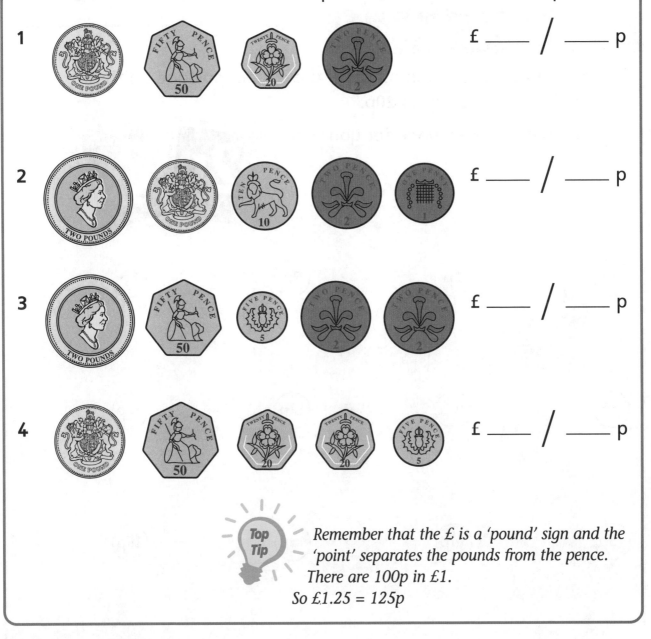

1   £ ____ / ____ p

2   £ ____ / ____ p

3   £ ____ / ____ p

4   £ ____ / ____ p

Top Tip — *Remember that the £ is a 'pound' sign and the 'point' separates the pounds from the pence. There are 100p in £1. So £1.25 = 125p*

Giving change

Write the change from £1 for each of these amounts.

1 65p → ____ p

2 40p → ____ p

3 85p → ____ p

4 15p → ____ p

5 79p → ____ p

6 54p → ____ p

Money investigation

What is the postage?

Using only 2p and 3p stamps, draw the correct postage on these postcards. Try to get up to 20p.

An example has been done for you.

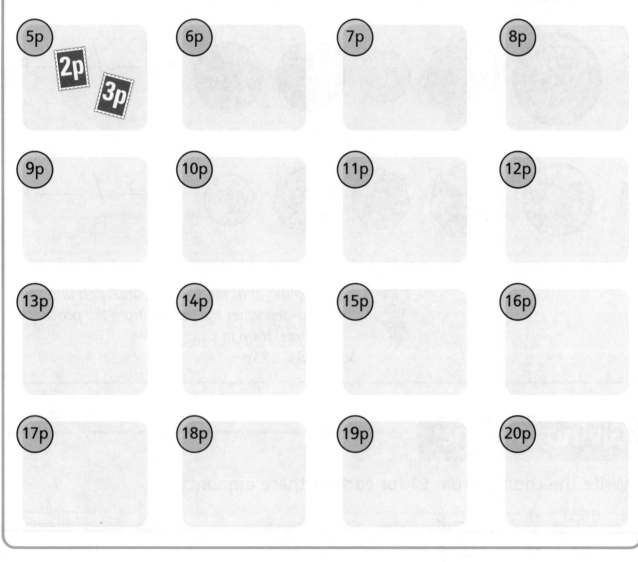

5p

6p

7p

8p

9p

10p

11p

12p

13p

14p

15p

16p

17p

18p

19p

20p

How many coins?

Look at each full purse, filling in the blanks to say how many coins there are and how much they add up to. Now draw the same amount of money in the empty purse, but only use half the number of coins.

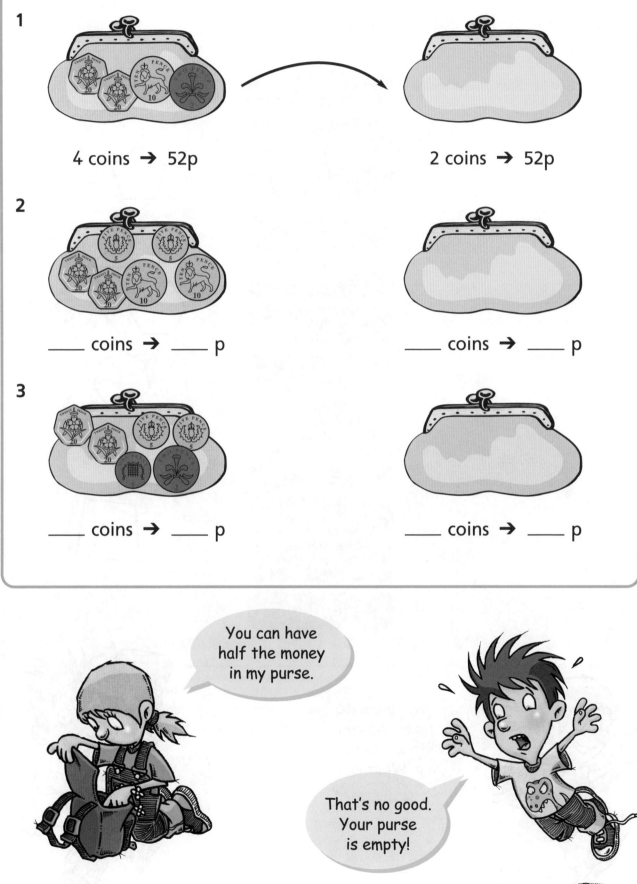

1

4 coins ➜ 52p

2 coins ➜ 52p

2

___ coins ➜ ___ p

___ coins ➜ ___ p

3

___ coins ➜ ___ p

___ coins ➜ ___ p

You can have half the money in my purse.

That's no good. Your purse is empty!

Shapes

Shape names

Draw a line to join each shape to its name.

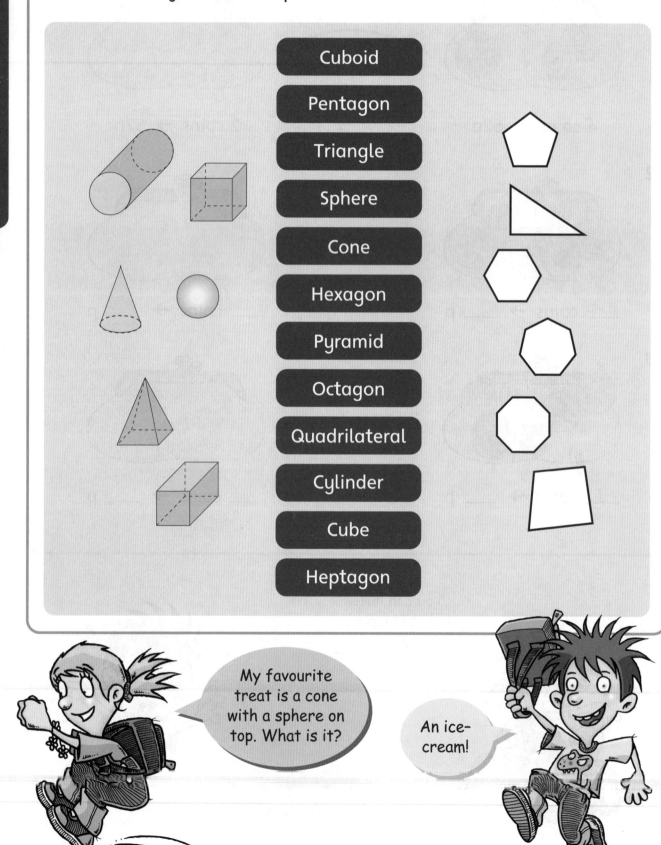

Cuboid

Pentagon

Triangle

Sphere

Cone

Hexagon

Pyramid

Octagon

Quadrilateral

Cylinder

Cube

Heptagon

My favourite treat is a cone with a sphere on top. What is it?

An ice-cream!

Answers

Numbers

PAGES 4–5 COUNTING PATTERNS

Counting objects

9 groups of 2 = **18** bugs

Counting to 100

0	1	2	3	4	**5**	6	7	**8**	9
10	11	**12**	**13**	**14**	15	16	**17**	18	19
20	21	**22**	23	**24**	25	**26**	27	28	**29**
30	**31**	32	33	34	**35**	36	**37**	38	**39**
40	**41**	42	**43**	**44**	45	**46**	47	48	49
50	51	**52**	**53**	54	55	56	**57**	**58**	**59**
60	61	**62**	63	**64**	**65**	**66**	**67**	68	69
70	71	**72**	73	74	75	**76**	77	**78**	79
80	**81**	82	**83**	84	**85**	86	**87**	88	**89**
90	**91**	92	**93**	94	95	**96**	**97**	**98**	99

Sequences

1 17, 18, **19**, **20**, 21, 22 , 23, **24**

2 46, **47**, 48, 49, **50**, **51**, 52, **53**

3 32, 31, **30**, 29, **28**, **27**, 26, **25**

4 **86**, **85**, 84, 83, **82**, 81, **80**, **79**

Number patterns

1 ⓪ 1 ② 3 ④ 5 ⑥ 7 ⑧ 9 ⑩ 11 ⑫ 13 ⑭ 15 ⑯ 17 ⑱ 19 ⑳

2 30, 35, 40, 45

3 12, 15, 18, 21

PAGES 6–7 READING AND WRITING NUMBERS

Teen numbers

	S	I	X	T	E	E	N		
			T	W	E	L	V	E	
	F	O	U	R	T	E	E	N	
			S	E	V	E	N	T	E	E	N
T	H	I	R	T	E	E	N		
			N	I	N	E	T	E	E	N

2-digit numbers

1 52	2 35	3 64	4 27
5 86	6 43	7 71	8 28

3-digit numbers

1 487 = **400** + 80 + 7

2 394 = 300 + **90** + 4

3 269 = **200** + 60 + 9

4 735 = **700** + 30 + 5

5 918 = **900** + 10 + 8

6 842 = 800 + **40** + 2

Odd and even numbers

Circled numbers are: 54, 50, 18, 26, 32.

Multiples

	multiple of 2	not a multiple of 2
multiple of 5	10 20 30 40	5 15 25 35
not a multiple of 5	2 4 6 8 12 14 16 18 22 24 26 28 32 34 36 38	1 3 7 9 11 13 17 19 21 23 27 29 31 33 37 39

They all end in zero.

PAGES 8–9 COMPARING AND ORDERING

Positions

Number sequence

1 17, **18**, **19**, **20**, **21**, **22**, **23**, 24

2 80, **79**, **78**, **77**, **76**, **75**, **74**, 73

3 43, **44**, **45**, **46**, **47**, **48**, **49**, 50

4 66, **65**, **64**, **63**, **62**, **61**, **60**, 59

Ordering numbers

1 19, 24, 25, 27, 30, 31

2 47, 52, 58, 60, 83, 85

Comparing numbers

1 34 ⑷⑶	2 ⑻⑴ 79	3 92 ⑼⑸	4 68 ⑻⑹
5 57 ⑹⑷	6 19 ⑼⑴	7 ⑺⑵ 69	8 ⑻⑺ 84

Halfway numbers

1 17 **21** 25	3 32 **35** 38
2 51 **54** 57	4 14 **20** 26

PAGES 10–11 ESTIMATING

Good estimates

Check child's estimate for accuracy.

Butterflies: count 34

Ladybirds: count 46

Tomatoes: count 17

Bananas: count 38

Number lines

1 4, 7   3 22, 29

2 11, 16   4 43, 47

Rounding

| 63p 55p 57p | 65p 66p 71p | 76p 81p 84p |
| Round to 60 | Round to 70 | Round to 80 |

PAGES 12–13 FRACTIONS

Fractions of shapes

1 any $\frac{1}{2}$ of each shape, for instance:

2 any $\frac{1}{4}$ of each shape, for instance:

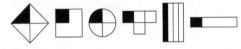

Equal parts

Ticked shapes are:

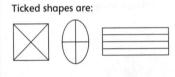

Fractions of amounts

1 3   5 2

2 5   6 3

3 4   7 5

4 6   8 4

PAGES 14–15 NUMBERS INVESTIGATION

Complete the square

100	99	98	97	96	95	94	93	92	91
90	89	88	87	86	85	84	83	82	81
80	79	78	77	76	75	74	73	72	71
70	69	68	67	66	65	64	63	62	61
60	59	58	57	56	55	54	53	52	51
50	49	48	47	46	45	44	43	42	41
40	39	38	37	36	35	34	33	32	31
30	29	28	27	26	25	24	23	22	21
20	19	18	17	16	15	14	13	12	11
10	9	8	7	6	5	4	3	2	1

And this one!

1	20	21	40	41	60	61	80	81	100
2	19	22	39	42	59	62	79	82	99
3	18	23	38	43	58	63	78	83	98
4	17	24	37	44	57	64	77	84	97
5	16	25	36	45	56	65	76	85	96
6	15	26	35	46	55	66	75	86	95
7	14	27	34	47	54	67	74	87	94
8	13	28	33	48	53	68	73	88	93
9	12	29	32	49	52	69	72	89	92
10	11	30	31	50	51	70	71	90	91

Calculations

PAGES 16–17 NUMBER FACTS

Totals to 10

9 = 4 + 5, 8 + 1, 0 + 9, 2 + 7, 3 + 6

10 = 3 + 7, 10 + 0, 6 + 4, 5 + 5, 2 + 8

Trios

1   4 + 7 = 11   11 − 7 = 4

    7 + 4 = 11   11 − 4 = 7

2   8 + 6 = 14   14 − 8 = 6

    6 + 8 = 14   14 − 6 = 8

3   9 + 7 = 16   16 − 9 = 7

    7 + 9 = 16   16 − 7 = 9

Number bonds

1 14, 11, 16, 16, 10, 17 = CARROT

2 17, 15, 16, 8, 13, 9 = TURNIP

3 9, 10, 17, 11, 17, 10 = POTATO

4 12, 9, 16, 10, 15, 17, 12 = SPROUTS

5 9, 11, 16, 12, 8, 13, 9 = PARSNIP

PAGES 18–19 ADDITION AND SUBTRACTION

Big numbers

1 50 → 130 → 110 → 160

2 80 → 30 → 120 → 40

3 500 → 300 → 1200 → 1900

4 700 → 800 → 300 → 200

Using doubles

1 28 29   4 70 71

2 42 43   5 50 49

3 120 119   6 80 81

Rounding

$14 + 19$ $17 - 9$ $46 - 19$ $23 + 9$ $15 + 9$ $26 - 9$

24 27 8 17 32 33

$27 - 19$ $42 - 9$ $33 - 9$ $36 - 19$ $13 + 19$ $18 + 9$

Adding 2-digit numbers

1	43	4	74
2	72	5	61
3	82	6	88

Counting on

1	9	4	14
2	14	5	19
3	17	6	19

PAGES 20–21 MULTIPLICATION AND DIVISION

Counting groups

1 $3 \times 4 = 12$
3 multiplied by 4 is **12**

2 $4 \times 5 = 20$
4 multiplied by 5 is **20**

Dividing

1 **6** groups of 2 $12 \div 2 = 6$
2 **5** groups of 3 $15 \div 3 = 5$
3 **4** groups of 4 $16 \div 4 = 4$
4 **4** groups of 3 $12 \div 3 = 4$
5 **3** groups of 5 $15 \div 5 = 3$
6 **3** groups of 4 $12 \div 4 = 3$

PAGES 22–23 TIMES TABLES

2 times table

1 ⓪ 1 ② 3 ④ 5 ⑥ 7 ⑧ 9 ⑩
11 ⑫ 13 ⑭ 15 ⑯ 17 ⑱ 19 ⑳

2 $4 \times 2 = 8$ $7 \times 2 = 14$ $2 \times 3 = 6$
   $5 \times 2 = 10$ $2 \times 9 = 18$ $8 \times 2 = 16$
   $10 \times 2 = 20$ $2 \times 2 = 4$ $2 \times 6 = 12$

Multiplying by 5 and 10

IN	3	9	8	5	7	6	2	4
OUT	15	45	**40**	25	**35**	30	**10**	20

IN	6	7	4	5	9	2	8	3
OUT	60	70	**40**	50	**90**	20	**80**	30

Multiplying by 3 and 4

1 15, 18, 21, 24, 27, 30
   20, 24, 28, 32, 36, 40

2 $3 \times 4 = 12$ $4 \times 8 = 32$ $2 \times 3 = 6$
   $5 \times 4 = 20$ $3 \times 7 = 21$ $4 \times 9 = 36$
   $9 \times 3 = 27$ $6 \times 4 = 24$ $8 \times 3 = 24$

Tricky tables

×	3	2	5
7	21	14	35
4	12	8	20
9	27	18	45

×	4	10	3
6	24	60	18
8	32	80	24
5	20	50	15

×	8	9	7
5	40	45	35
3	24	27	21
4	32	36	28

PAGES 24–25 PROBLEM-SOLVING

Word problems

1	90 cm	4	9 eggs
2	9 stickers	5	7 sweets
3	4 cars	6	14 kg

Money totals

1 £1.72 / 172p   3 £2.59 / 259p
2 £3.13 / 313p   4 £1.95 / 195p

Giving change

1	35p	4	85p
2	60p	5	21p
3	15p	6	46p

PAGES 26–27 MONEY INVESTIGATION

What is the postage?

Many answers are possible. Check child's answers.

How many coins?

1
50p and 2p

2
6 coins → 70p   3 coins → 70p

3
6 coins → 53p   3 coins → 53p

Shapes and measures

PAGES 28-29 SHAPES
Shape names

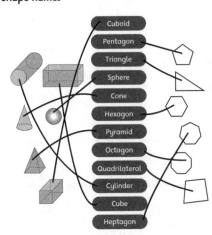

Cuboid
Pentagon
Triangle
Sphere
Cone
Hexagon
Pyramid
Octagon
Quadrilateral
Cylinder
Cube
Heptagon

Sorting shapes

1

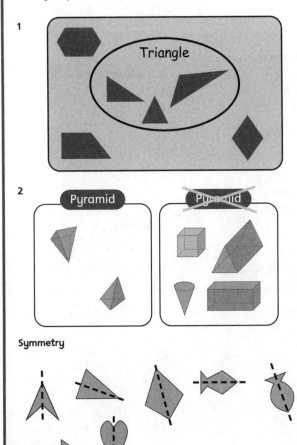

Triangle

2

Pyramid   ~~Pyramid~~

Symmetry

Right angles

Directions

1	park	3	church
2	church	4	park

Points of the compass

NORTH

WEST ←→ EAST

SOUTH

PAGES 32–33 MEASUREMENT
Units of measurement

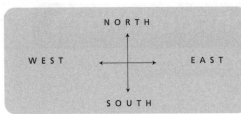

Centimetres
Metres
Millilitres
Litres
Grams
Kilograms

30kg

Heavier or lighter?

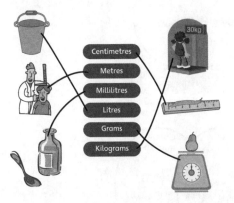

Longer or shorter?

Check child's estimates for accuracy.

Exact lengths

1	3 cm	4	7 cm
2	5 cm	5	9 cm
3	6 cm		

PAGES 34–35 TIME
Time facts

1	60 minutes = 1 hour	7 days = 1 week
	12 months = 1 year	60 seconds = 1 minute
	24 hours = 1 day	52 weeks = 1 year

PAGES 30–31 POSITION AND TURNING
Grids

1	B6 → car	A4 → cat
	E2 → horse	B3 → tree

2   → B1   → D4

→ F5   → D6

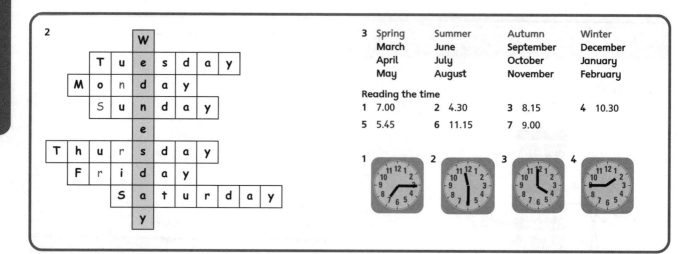

2

			W					
	T	u	e	s	d	a	y	
M	o	n	d	a	y			
	S	u	n	d	a	y		
			e					
T	h	u	r	s	d	a	y	
F	r	i	d	a	y			
	S	a	t	u	r	d	a	y
			y					

3

Spring	Summer	Autumn	Winter
March	June	September	December
April	July	October	January
May	August	November	February

Reading the time

1 7.00   2 4.30   3 8.15   4 10.30
5 5.45   6 11.15   7 9.00

1   2   3   4

Graphs and charts

PAGES 38–39 SORTING DIAGRAMS

Venn diagrams

1

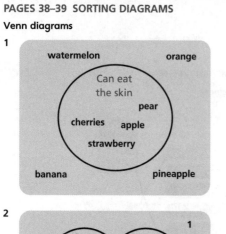

2

watermelon   orange

Can eat the skin

pear
cherries   apple
strawberry

banana   pineapple

Even numbers / Greater than 10

Carroll diagrams

Tree diagrams

1   18 → B   2   65 → C   3   7 → A
4   94 → D   5   100 → D   6   21 → A

PAGES 40–41 READING GRAPHS

Pictograms

1 9   4 David and Katy
2 Ben   5 12
3 7   6 3

Block graphs

1 5   3 11
2 3   4 28

Bar charts

1 Tuesday   3 6
2 9   4 Monday

PAGES 42–43 GRAPHS INVESTIGATION

Check child's results.

National Test practice

PAGES 44–49 TEST 1

1 37p

2
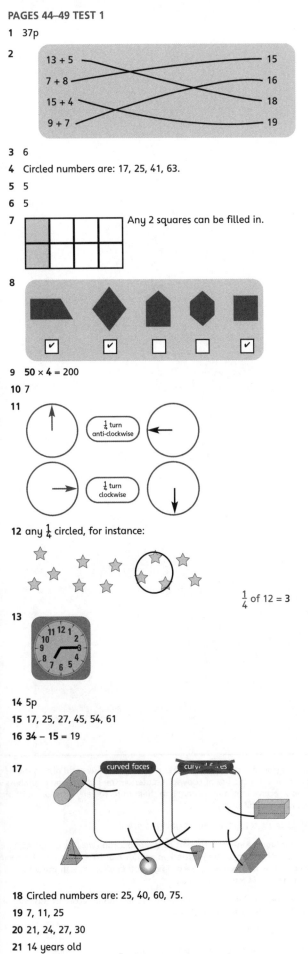

13 + 5 ⟶ 15
7 + 8 ⟶ 16
15 + 4 ⟶ 18
9 + 7 ⟶ 19

3 6

4 Circled numbers are: 17, 25, 41, 63.

5 5

6 5

7 Any 2 squares can be filled in.

8 ☑ ☑ ☐ ☐ ☑

9 50 × 4 = 200

10 7

11
¼ turn anti-clockwise

¼ turn clockwise

12 any ¼ circled, for instance:

¼ of 12 = 3

13

14 5p

15 17, 25, 27, 45, 54, 61

16 34 − 15 = 19

17
curved faces   curved faces

18 Circled numbers are: 25, 40, 60, 75.

19 7, 11, 25

20 21, 24, 27, 30

21 14 years old

22 104

23 74, 59

24 607

25 33, 36, 39

PAGES 50–54 TEST 2

1 20, 23, 26

2 Monday

3 33

4 Thursday

5

6 3

7
North
West   East
South

8

9 6

10 13 + 8 + 9 = 30

11 3 coins: 50p, 20p, 20p

12 £14

13

×	2	10	4
3	6	30	12
5	10	50	20
2	4	20	8

14 27

15
Triangles

16 150

17 9

18 121

19 103

20 5

21 2 km

22 £20

23 b

24 25

25 1500 ml

Letts Educational
The Chiswick Centre, 414 Chiswick High Road, London W4 5TF
Tel: 0845 602 1937
Fax: 020 8742 8390
E-mail: mail@lettsed.co.uk

Website: www.letts-successzone.com

First published 2007

Editorial and design: 2ibooks [publishing solutions] Cambridge

Colour Reprographics by PDQ

Author: Paul Broadbent
Book concept and development: Helen Jacobs, Publishing Director
Project editor: Lily Morgan
Illustrator: Piers Baker
Cover design: Angela English

British Library Cataloging in Publication Data. A CIP record of this book is available from the British Library.

9781843157441

Printed in Italy

Sorting shapes

Draw the shapes in the correct parts of each diagram.

1

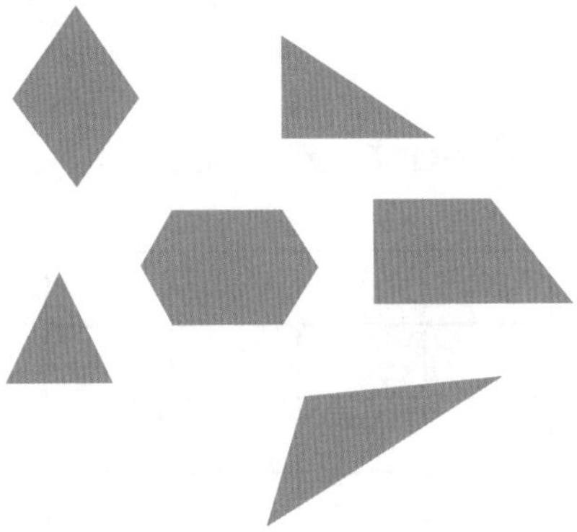

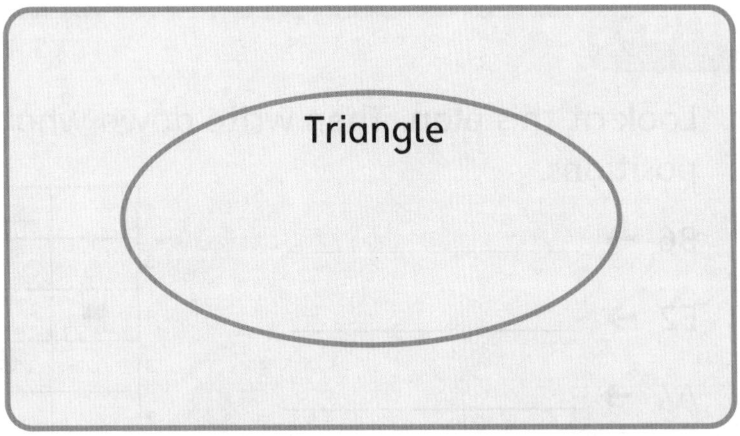

Triangle

2

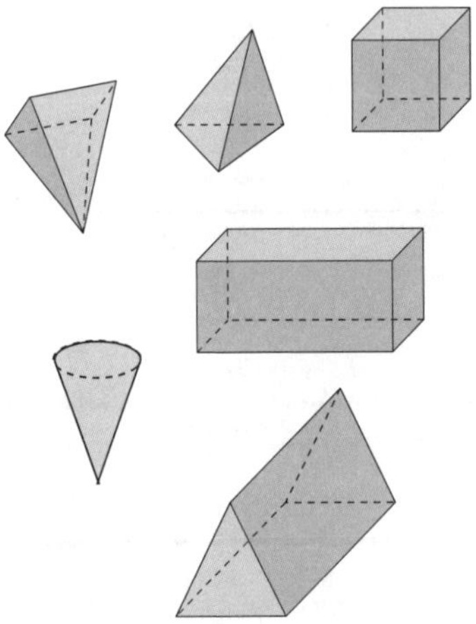

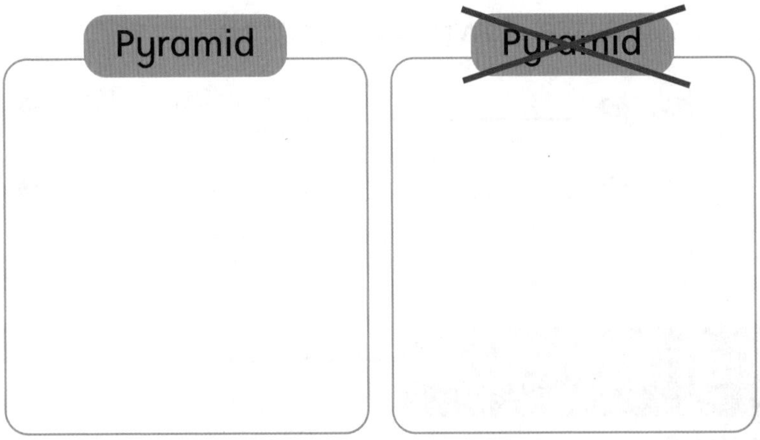

Pyramid

~~Pyramid~~

Symmetry

Draw a line of symmetry on each shape.

Top Tip

A line of symmetry is like a fold line. If you imagine a symmetrical shape folded down the middle, the two sides would match.

Position and turning

Grids

1   Look at this plan. Then write down what is at each of these positions.

    B6 → _____

    E2 → _____

    A4 → _____

    B3 → _____

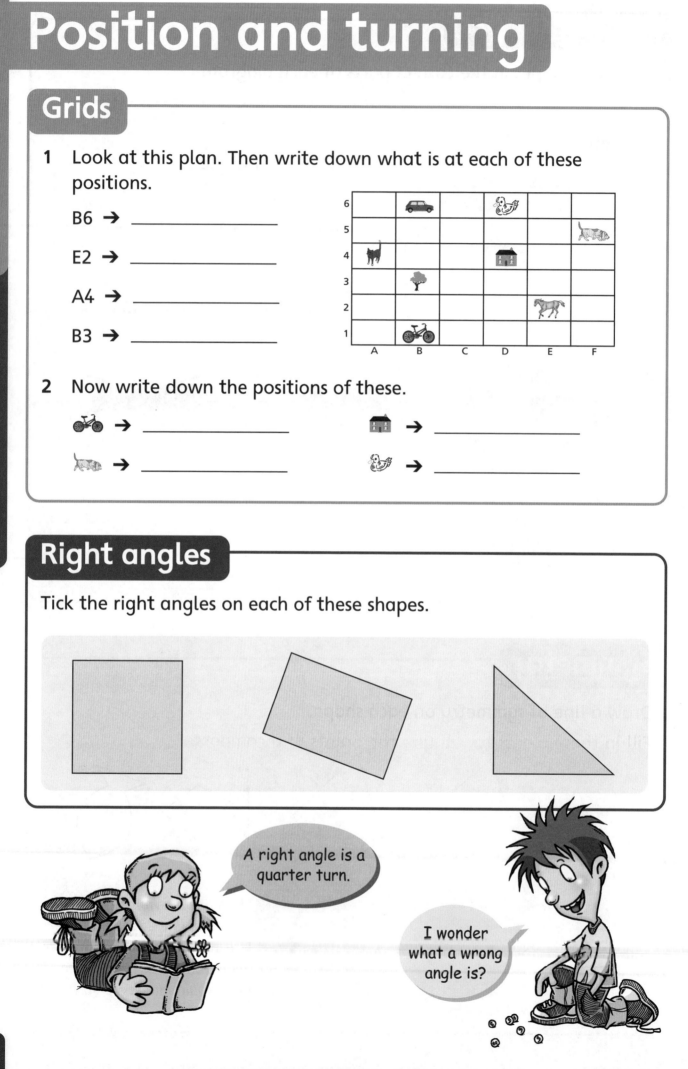

2   Now write down the positions of these.

    🚲 → _____   🏠 → _____

    🐕 → _____   🦆 → _____

Right angles

Tick the right angles on each of these shapes.

A right angle is a quarter turn.

I wonder what a wrong angle is?

Directions

Write down where Sam will be facing after these turns.

	Start position	Turn	Finish position
1	Facing the church	$\frac{1}{4}$ turn clockwise	_____
2	Facing the park	$\frac{1}{4}$ turn anti-clockwise	_____
3	Facing the school	$\frac{1}{2}$ turn clockwise	_____
4	Facing home	$\frac{1}{2}$ turn anti-clockwise	_____

Top Tip *Remember, clockwise moves in the direction of clock hands and anti-clockwise goes in the opposite direction.*

Points of the compass

Fill in these words to tell you the points of a compass.

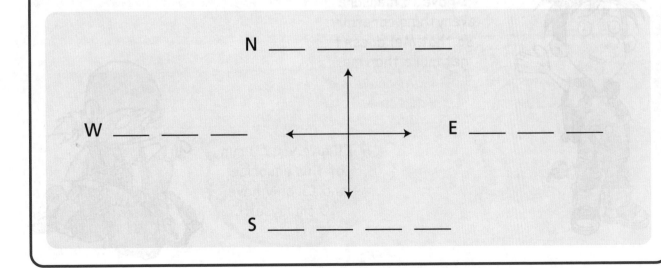

N __ __ __ __

W __ __ __

E __ __ __

S __ __ __ __

Measurement

Units of measurement

Draw a line to join each item to the correct unit of measurement.

I have to measure everything carefully so that Mel doesn't get more than me.

I'll give you 50 mm of this liquorice and I'll only have 10 cm myself!

Heavier or lighter?

Circle the objects that you think weigh more than 1 kilogram.

Longer or shorter?

How long do you think that each of these pencils is? First, write down your estimate. Then measure the pencil for the exact length.

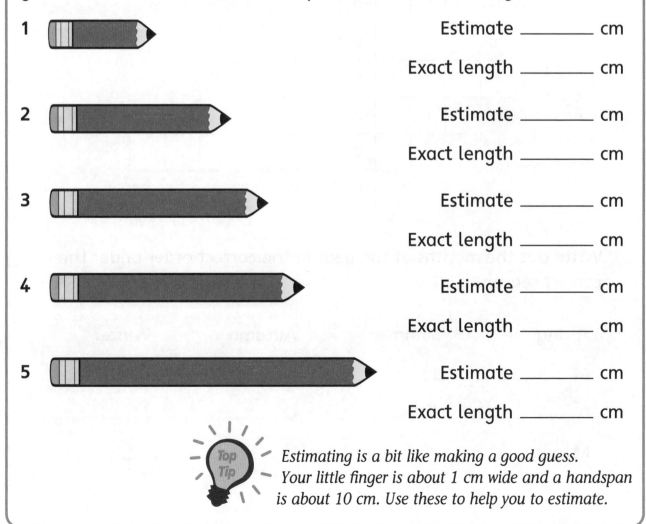

1   Estimate _____ cm

Exact length _____ cm

2   Estimate _____ cm

Exact length _____ cm

3   Estimate _____ cm

Exact length _____ cm

4   Estimate _____ cm

Exact length _____ cm

5   Estimate _____ cm

Exact length _____ cm

Top Tip

Estimating is a bit like making a good guess. Your little finger is about 1 cm wide and a handspan is about 10 cm. Use these to help you to estimate.

Time

Time facts

1 Fill in the missing information about times.

_____ minutes = 1 hour   _____ days = 1 week

_____ months = 1 year   _____ seconds = 1 minute

_____ hours = 1 day   _____ weeks = 1 year

2 Complete this puzzle grid by writing in the other six days of the week.

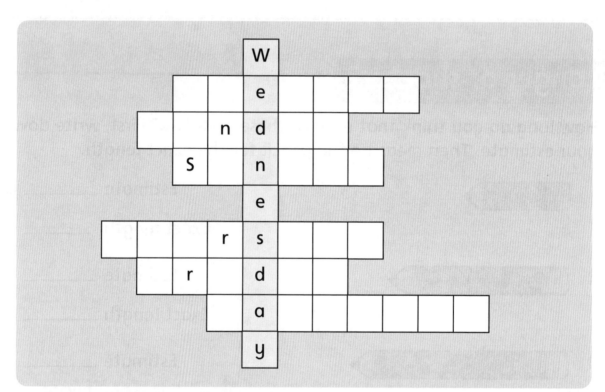

3 Write out the months of the year in the correct order under the correct season.

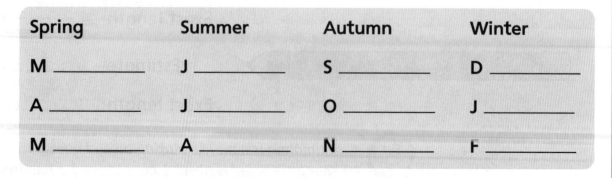

Spring	Summer	Autumn	Winter
M _____	J _____	S _____	D _____
A _____	J _____	O _____	J _____
M _____	A _____	N _____	F _____

Reading the time

Write down the times shown on each of these clocks.

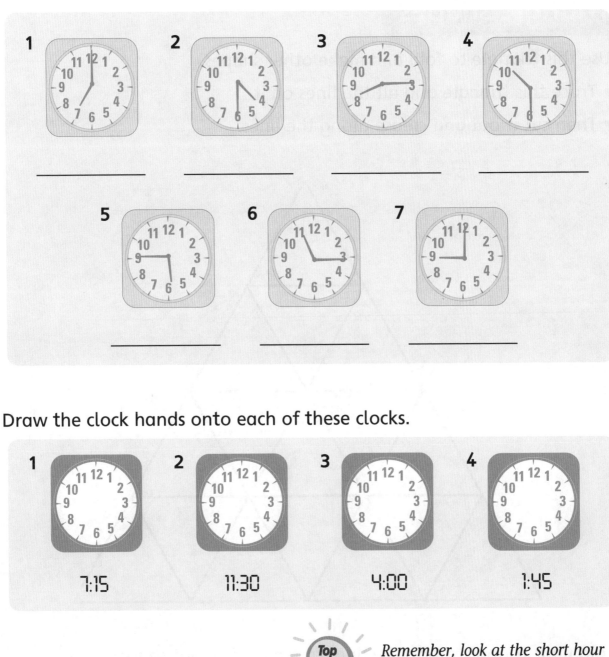

1 _____   2 _____   3 _____   4 _____

5 _____   6 _____   7 _____

Draw the clock hands onto each of these clocks.

1   7:15   2   11:30   3   4:00   4   1:45

Top Tip Remember, look at the short hour hand first and then count the number of minutes past the hour.

What has a face and hands but no eyes and no arms?

A clock!

Shapes investigation

Triangle shapes

Use this triangle to fold and make other shapes.

• Trace this triangle and all the lines on it.

• Then cut it out and crease along the lines.

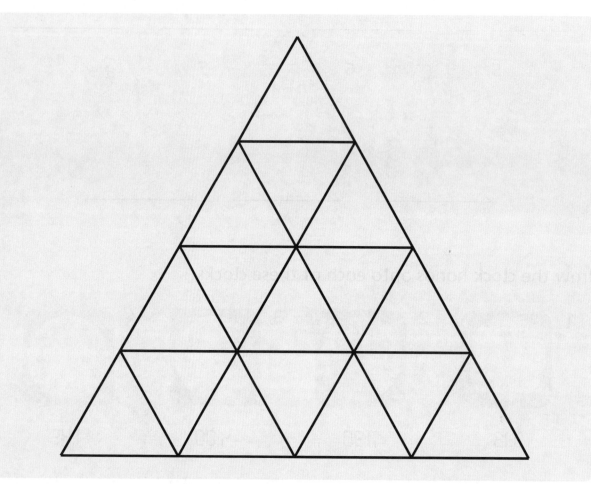

Fold your triangle along the lines to make different shapes.

Different shapes

Now use your triangle to make these shapes.

1 Two different quadrilaterals

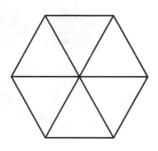
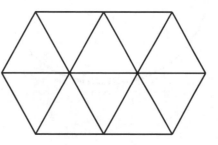

2 Two different hexagons

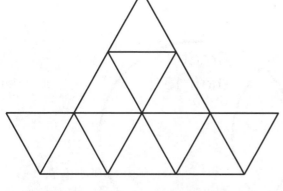

3 A boat

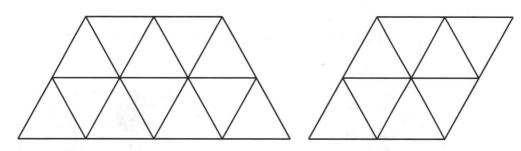

Keep playing with your triangle to see what other shapes you can make.

That boat is a heptagon.

A 7-sided boat to sail the 7 seas!

Sorting diagrams

Venn diagrams

1 Sort the fruit by writing the names on this Venn diagram.

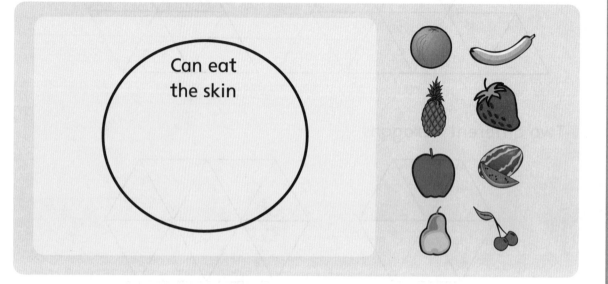

Can eat the skin

2 Write the numbers 1 to 20 on this Venn diagram.

Even numbers

Greater than 10

How can you make a LEMON double in size?

Change its letters to make it a MELON!

Carroll diagrams

Draw these shapes on this Carroll diagram.

Four sides	~~Four sides~~

Top Tip *In Carroll diagrams, one 'label' is always the opposite of another. So this has 'four sides' and 'not four sides' as the labels. The crossing out shows that shapes that do not have four sides go in this part of the diagram.*

Tree diagrams

Look at this tree diagram.

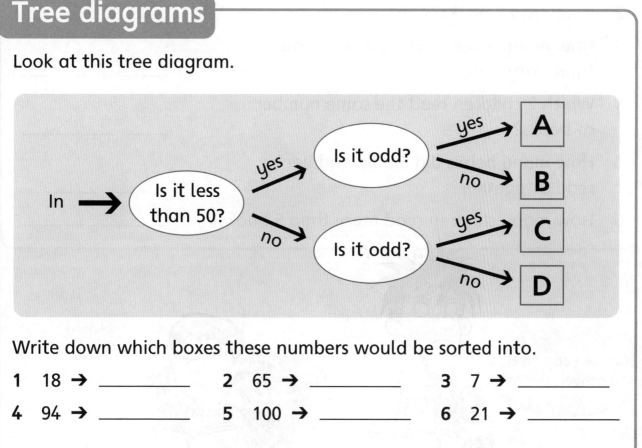

Write down which boxes these numbers would be sorted into.

1 18 → _____   **2** 65 → _____   **3** 7 → _____

4 94 → _____   **5** 100 → _____   **6** 21 → _____

Reading graphs

Pictograms

This pictogram shows the number of books read by a group of children in one month.

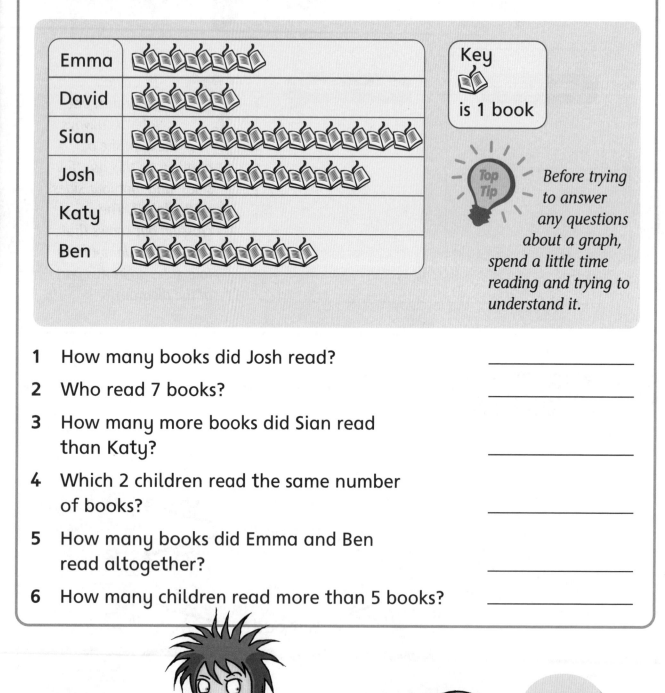

Key

📖 is 1 book

Top Tip Before trying to answer any questions about a graph, spend a little time reading and trying to understand it.

1   How many books did Josh read? _____

2   Who read 7 books? _____

3   How many more books did Sian read than Katy? _____

4   Which 2 children read the same number of books? _____

5   How many books did Emma and Ben read altogether? _____

6   How many children read more than 5 books? _____

How do you travel to school, Mel?

Slowly!

Block graphs

This graph shows how a class of children travel to school.

Key

is 1 child

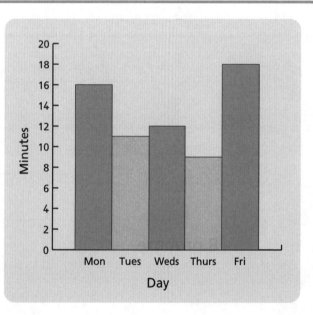

1   How many children travelled by car? ____

2   How many more children walked than cycled? ____

3   How many children did not walk or cycle? ____

4   How many children are there altogether in the class? ____

Bar charts

This graph shows the time Daniel took to travel to school each day for a week.

1   On which day did he take 11 minutes? _____

2   How many minutes was his journey on Thursday? _____

3   How much longer did it take him to travel on Friday than on Wednesday? _____

4   Which day took 5 minutes longer than travelling on Tuesday? _____

Graphs investigation

Gathering information

- Choose one of your reading books and open it on any page.

- Count the number of letters for each of the words on the page. For example, the word GRAPH has 5 letters.

- Keep a tally to show the number of words with 1 letter, the number of words with 2 letters, and so on. Your tally will be easier to count if you use IIII.

Number of letters	Tally of words
1	
2	
3	
4	
5	
6	
7	
8 or more	

Top Tip *Draw the tally in groups of 5. IIII shows 5. It makes it easy to count.*

Plotting your graph

Draw a bar graph to show the number of words for each letter count. Use your tally chart opposite to draw the graph. Decide on the scale of your graph.

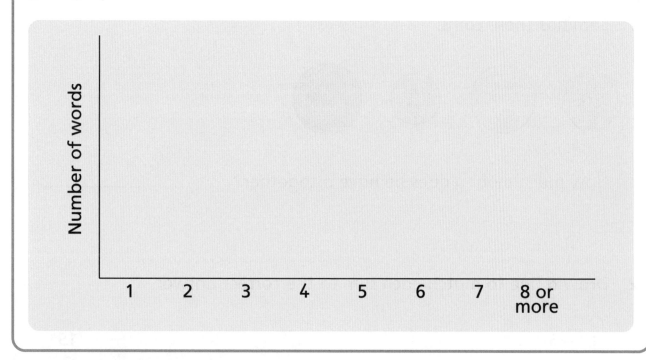

Number of words

1   2   3   4   5   6   7   8 or more

Using your graph

Use your graph to answer these questions.

1   What is the most common length of word?   _____

2   What is the least common length of word?   _____

Can you make a sentence with only 3-letter words?

Mel and Sam ate ham and red jam for tea!

National Test practice

Test 1

1 Sam has these coins:

How much money does he have altogether? _____

2 Draw a line to match each sum to the correct answer.

13 + 5	15
7 + 8	16
15 + 4	18
9 + 7	19

3 Write in the missing number.

14 − ☐ = 8

4 Draw a circle round each odd number.

14 17 25 34 41 50 63

5 This graph shows the favourite fruit of a group of children.

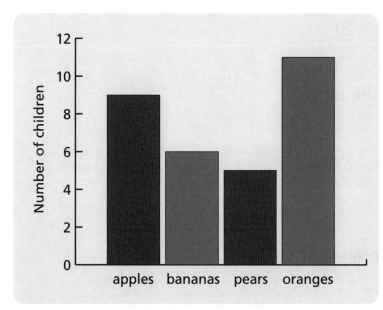

How many children chose pears? _____

6 How many more children chose oranges
than bananas? _____

7 Colour $\frac{1}{4}$ of this shape.

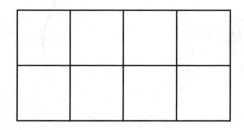

8 Tick the quadrilaterals.

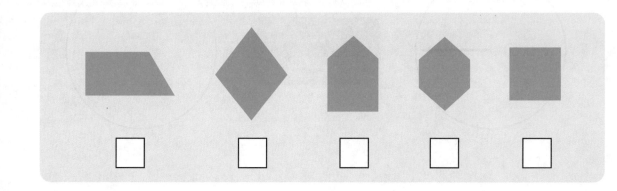

9 Use 2 of these numbers to make 200.

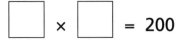

50   8   100   4   20

Write the numbers in the boxes.

☐ × ☐ = 200

10 2 numbers have a difference of 15.

The larger number is 22.

Write down the other number.   _____

11 Draw an arrow to show each turn.

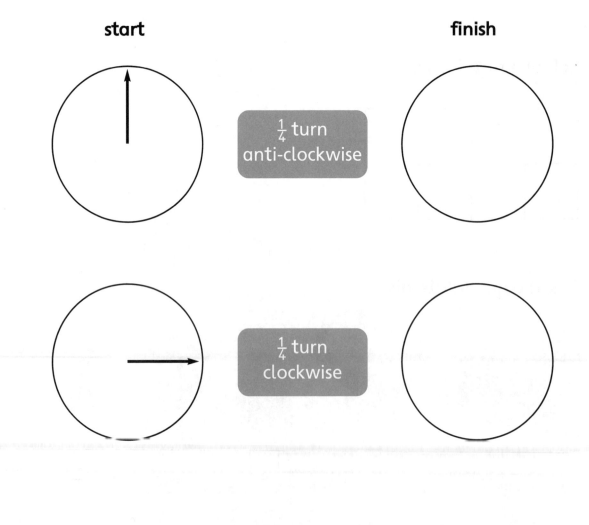

start   finish

¼ turn
anti-clockwise

¼ turn
clockwise

12 Draw a circle round $\frac{1}{4}$ of these stars.

$\frac{1}{4}$ of 12 = ☐

13 A film started at 7.15pm.

Draw in the hands on this clockface to show the time.

14 An ice-lolly costs 15p.

Laura buys 3 ice-lollies.

What change does she get from 50p? _____

15 Write these numbers in order, starting with the smallest.

27   45   17   54   61   25

___   ___   ___   ___   ___   ___

16 Write down 2 of these numbers to make 19.

34   51   46   28   15

☐ – ☐ = 19

17 Draw a line to join these shapes to the correct box.

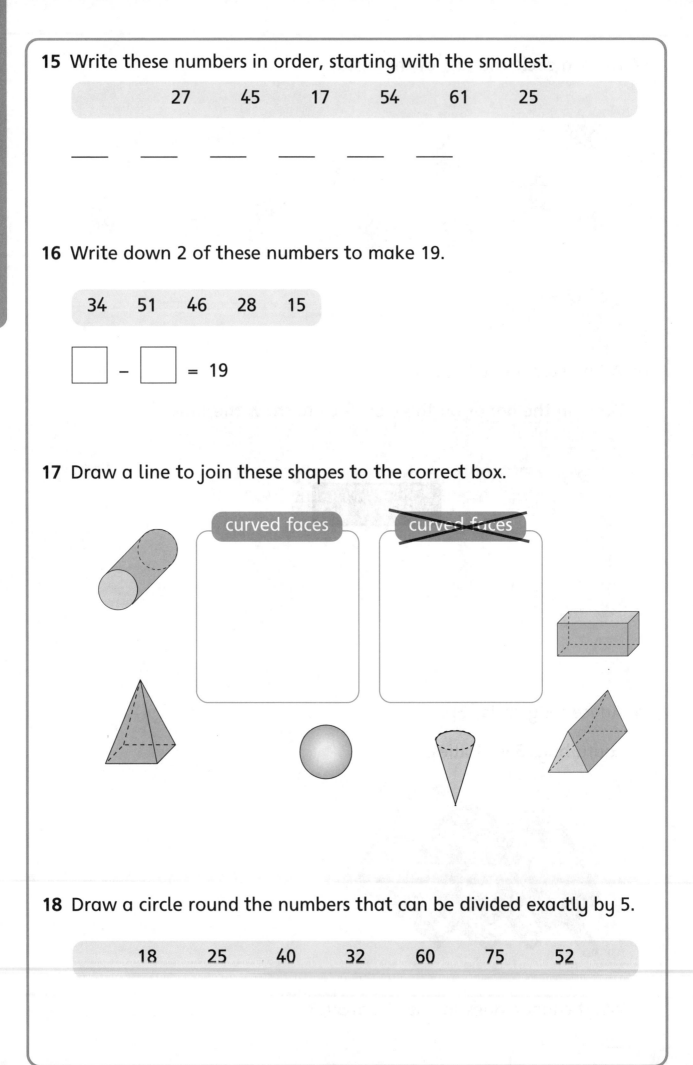

curved faces   ~~curved faces~~

18 Draw a circle round the numbers that can be divided exactly by 5.

18   25   40   32   60   75   52

19 Fill in the boxes to show which numbers went into this machine.

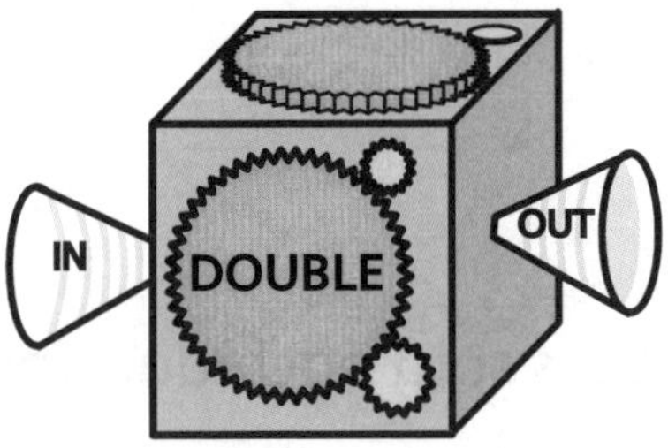

DOUBLE
IN   OUT

14

22

50

20 Fill in the boxes to continue this pattern.

9   12   15   18

21 Laura has a brother, Josh, who is double her age.

If he is 7 years older than Laura, how old is Josh? _____

22 Write the total.

$38 + 47 + 19 =$ ☐

23 Write the missing numbers in this sequence.

84   79   ☐   69   64   ☐

24 Write the number that is 100 more than 507. _____

25 Which multiples of 3 are between 32 and 40?

_____

Test 2

1 What are the next three numbers in this sequence?

8   11   14   17   ☐   ☐   ☐

This chart shows the number of pizzas sold each day for a week from 'The Pizza Place'.

Monday	Tuesday	Wednesday	Thursday	Friday	Saturday	Sunday
48	54	87	79	96	118	62

2 On which day were the fewest pizzas sold? _____

3 How many more pizzas were sold on Wednesday than on Tuesday? _____

4 On which day were approximately 80 pizzas sold? _____

5 Draw a line of symmetry on this triangle.

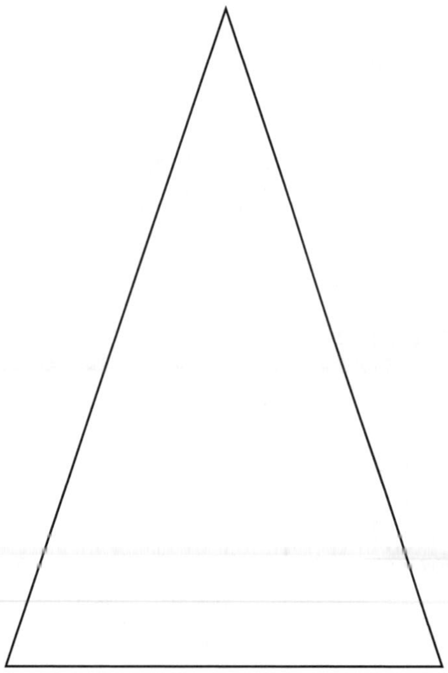

6 There are three types of fish in a pond: Goldfish, Koi and Tench. Half of the fish are Goldfish and four of the fish are Koi. If there are 14 fish altogether, how many Tench are there?

_____

7 Complete the missing points on this compass.

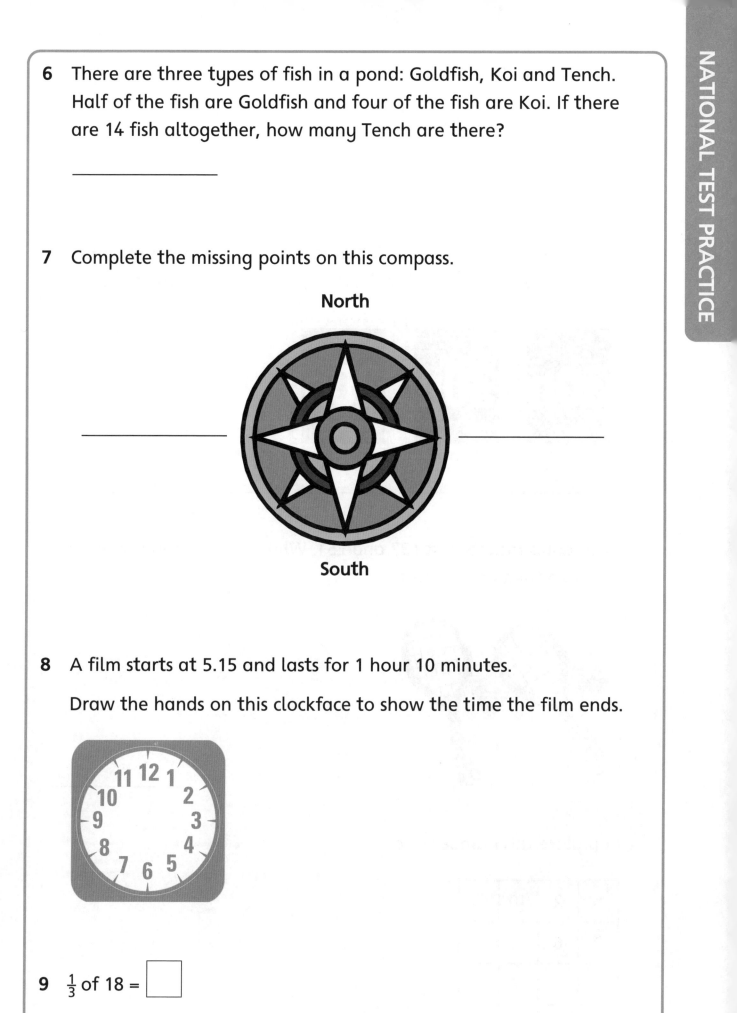

North

_____   _____

South

8 A film starts at 5.15 and lasts for 1 hour 10 minutes.

Draw the hands on this clockface to show the time the film ends.

9 $\frac{1}{3}$ of 18 = ▢

10 Use three of these numbers to make this correct.

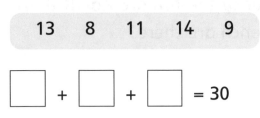

13   8   11   14   9

☐ + ☐ + ☐ = 30

11 Three stamps cost 30p each. What is the fewest number of coins that can be used to pay for the stamps exactly? List the coins:

_____

12 Two tennis rackets cost £37 and £51. What is the difference in price between the two rackets?

_____

13 Complete this number grid.

×	2	10	
3	6		
		50	
2			8

14 Jamie has 9 marbles and Becky has twice as many. How many marbles have they got altogether? _____

15 Draw these shapes on this Venn diagram.

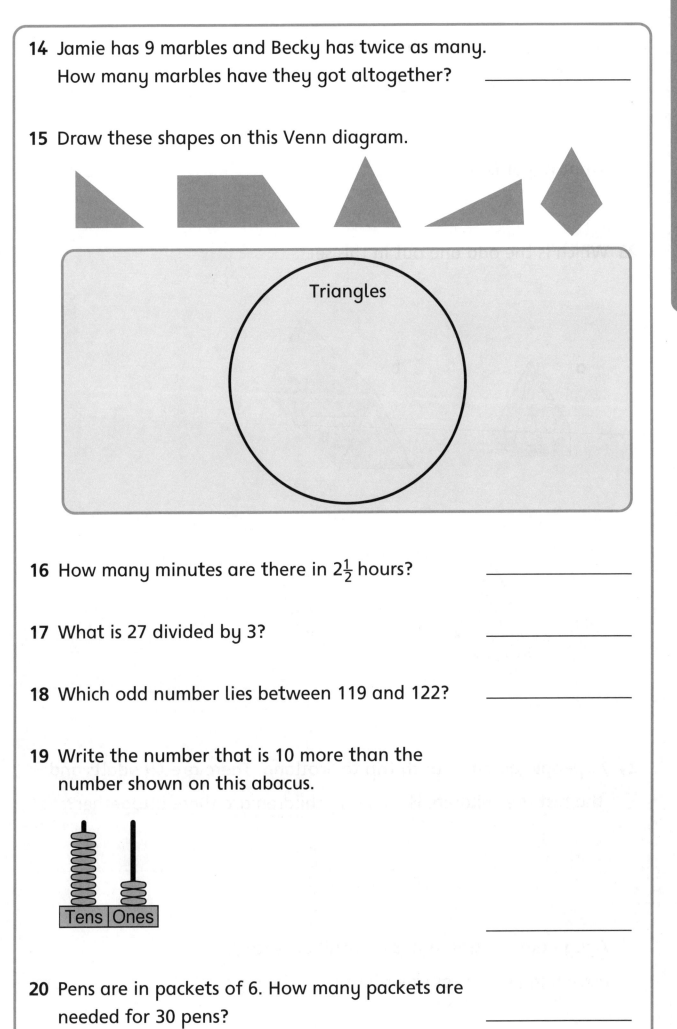

Triangles

16 How many minutes are there in $2\frac{1}{2}$ hours? _____

17 What is 27 divided by 3? _____

18 Which odd number lies between 119 and 122? _____

19 Write the number that is 10 more than the number shown on this abacus.

Tens | Ones

_____

20 Pens are in packets of 6. How many packets are needed for 30 pens? _____

21 Underline the length that is the greatest.

    240 mm   2 km   300 m   7 cm

22 What is $\frac{1}{4}$ of £80?   _____

23 Which is the odd one out in this set?

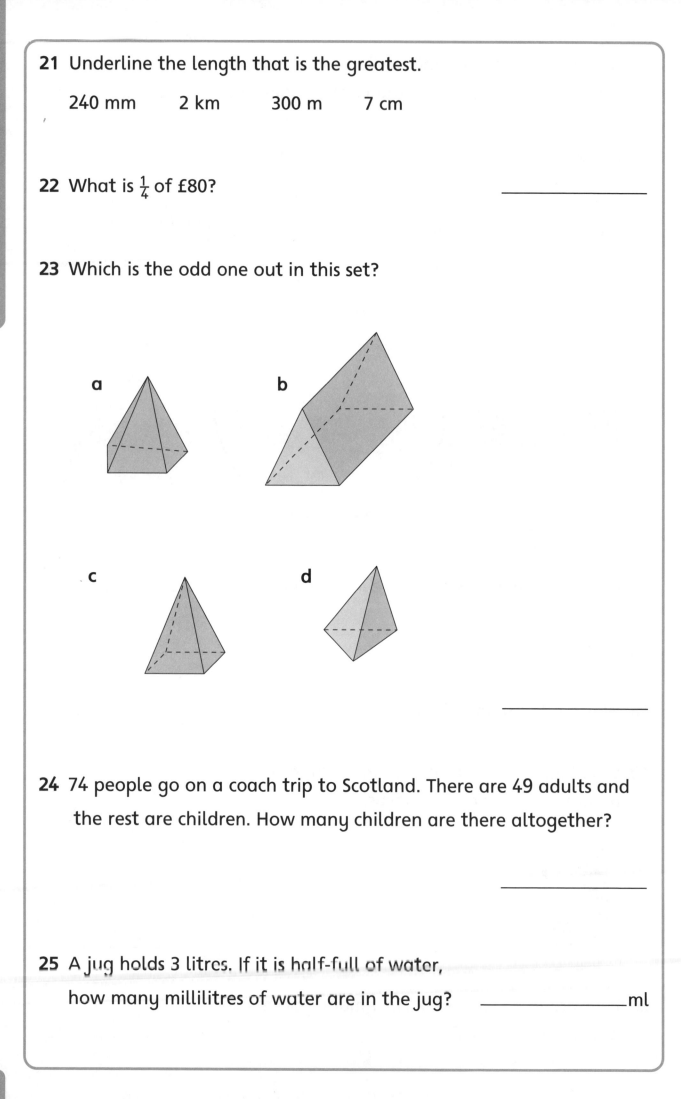

a

b

c

d

_____

24 74 people go on a coach trip to Scotland. There are 49 adults and the rest are children. How many children are there altogether?

_____

25 A jug holds 3 litres. If it is half-full of water, how many millilitres of water are in the jug?   _____ml

anti-clockwise turning in this direction, opposite to the hands of a clock

approximate a 'rough' answer - near to the real answer

axis (plural: axes) the horizontal (x) and vertical (y) lines on a graph

bar chart a type of graph that has bars to show amounts

block graph a type of graph where each block means one amount

calculation adding, taking away, multiplying and dividing are all calculations

capacity the amount of liquid a container holds

Carroll diagram a sorting diagram that shows groups of things in a grid

clockwise turning in this direction, like the hands of a clock

corner where the edges or sides of shapes meet

difference the amount by which one number is greater than another, e.g. the difference between 9 and 14 is 5

digits there are 10 digits: 0 1 2 3 4 5 6 7 8 and 9 that make all the numbers we use

divide share or group; ÷ is the sign for divide

double make something twice as big, or multiply by 2

dozen another word for twelve

edge where two faces of a solid shape meet

estimate a good guess

even numbers numbers that can be divided exactly by 2. They end in 0, 2, 4, 6 or 8

face the flat side of a solid shape

fraction part of a whole one

half $\frac{1}{2}$ is one half, or one out of two parts

heptagon a shape with 7 straight sides

hexagon a shape with 6 straight sides

length how long an object is

multiples a number made by multiplying together two other numbers

octagon a shape with 8 straight sides

odd numbers numbers that cannot be divided exactly by 2; odd numbers always end in 1, 3, 5, 7 or 9

pentagon a shape with 5 straight sides

pictogram graphs that use symbols or pictures, where each symbol represents a certain number of items

quadrilateral a shape with 4 straight sides

right angle a quarter turn; the corner of a square is a right angle

rounding changing a number to the nearest ten; a 'round number' is a number ending in zero: 10, 20, 30, 40, 50, 60, 70, 80, 90 or 100

scale the labelled marks that show an amount on rulers, jugs and weighing scales, etc.

sequence a list of numbers which usually have a pattern, often written in order

square a shape with four equal sides

symmetrical when two halves of a shape or pattern are identical

total when you add numbers together, the answer is the total

triangle a shape with 3 straight sides

Venn diagram a way of showing how different things can be sorted into groups, called sets

weight how heavy an object is

zero 0 or nothing